Who Lifted the Lid Off of Hell?

Who Lifted The Lid Off of HELL

?

Price

All war
is suicide for the
people who
began it

Who Lifted The Lid Off of HELL

?

By Elbert Hubbard

Who Lifted
The Lid Off of Hell?

By Elbert Hubbard

THE one intent of modern commerce is to bestow a benefit ✒ The one intent of war is to intimidate, cripple, maim and destroy ✒ Commerce stands for health and happiness.

War symbols suffering and disease.

Commerce is equitable exchange, and the more your business can be placed on a friendly basis, the better.

Commerce spells reciprocity, mutuality, co-operation ✒ ✒

We make money out of our friends. Our enemies will not trade with us if they can help it—and they usually can.

Business means food, clothing, shelter, trees, flowers, schools, savings-banks,

3

wages—with opportunities for education and promotion.

———

THE Hanseatic League, four hundred years ago, made war on pirates. It cleared the sea of buccaneers and made shipping safe.

In the same way cities now free themselves from highwaymen and burglars, in order that commodities may flow full and free, from where they are plentiful to where they are needed.

War as a corrective for industrial jealousy would be like making love with a bludgeon, managing a kindergarten with a black-snake whip, or introducing hope, faith and charity with the aid of thumbscrews.

A " successful " war is a contradiction in terms ❧ ❧

War destroys your market, limits your territory, lessens your prospects; and the

4

more " successful " the war, the more it kills the buying ability of your customers. ¶ All war—whether successful or not—destroys productive power.

And worst of all, it smothers good-will, kills credit, stampedes confidence—things that constitute the nervous system of the business body.

———

IF you will examine the present European war situation carefully, you will find it stamped and stenciled, " Made in Germany."

The charitable view is to assume that the War-Lord is a subject for the pathologist and the alienist.

He is a warrior first and forever.

A thousand photographs reveal him belted, booted, bespurred for slaughter.

These pictures attest his vanity in braid

5

and buttons, and show his love for glittering steel.

He symbols Mars, not Mercury.

———

THE soldier at best is a night-watchman.
¶ At worst, unchecked, he is a wild, weird, woolly head-hunter.

The fallacy of allowing a night-watchman to dictate business policies is now apparent.

¶ A night-watchman must be made to ring up; otherwise, he will get the idea in his head that he is owner of the plant.

Suppose we exalt our police system into a court from which there is no appeal, putting the night-watchman in as general manager of our factories, stores, railroads, allowing him to transform his billy into a scepter—could civilization exist?

Militarism must be shorn of its buttons, clipped of its power, in order that men may work, and work in peace.

6

" Safety First " demands that Kruppism
get the blue envelope ; and the sooner this
happens, the better it will be for the commerce of the world.

IF any one asks, " Who lifted the lid off
of Hell?" let the truthful answer be,
" William Hohenzollern."

Had this man used his power for peace
instead of invading a neutral country, there
would have been no war.

England would have joined with Germany
in checking Austria's belligerency.

But Wilhelm wanted war, and war he has.

He it was who used the bung-starter.

"Bill Kaiser" has a withered hand and
a running ear.

Also, he has a shrunken soul, and a mind
that reeks with egomania.

He is a mastoid degenerate of a noble
grandmother ❧ ❧

7

In degree he has her power, but not her
love. He has her persistence, but not her
prescience ✸ ✸

He is swollen, like a drowned pup, with a
pride that stinks.

He never wrote a letter or a message where-
in he did not speak of God as if the Creator
was waiting to see him in the lobby. " God
is with us "—" God is destroying our enemies "—" I am praying our God to be with
you "—" God is giving us victories "—" I
am accountable only to my conscience and
to God."

This belief that the Maker of the Universe
takes a special interest in him marks the
man as a megalomaniac; and the idea
that the nations were " laying for him " is
the true symptom of paranoia.

His talk of a Slav invasion is stall stuff,
subtle and sly, to divert attention from his
own crafty designs.

8

Is a Slav invasion more to be dreaded than a Germanic? Ask Belgium !

THE War-God's interest in farming was a pose—his encouragement of business a subterfuge.

Every farmer between fourteen and sixty years of age has been drafted into the ranks to be food for vultures.

Every farm-horse that could carry a man or draw a load has been seized.

All beef-cattle have been appropriated.

Every penny in every savings-bank in Germany has been levied upon, and a " receipt " given to the starving holder. The loss of a lifetime's savings means death to a multitude of old people, to widows, children, invalids and cripples.

The money a man might have left to care for his widow, orphans, aged parents, is swept away in the maelstrom of blood.

¶ Old-age pensions, sick benefits, and life-insurance are only dreams.

We are told that the Kaiser kept the peace for forty-three years. True—just waiting for this stroke at world dominion.

Every male child born in that forty-three years, who can carry a gun, is taken from useful work, and made to do the obscene bidding of this sad, mad, bad, bloody monster ✍ ✍

In Germany no private individual can operate an automobile. All the oil and "petrol" has been seized to incinerate the dead. No slab marks their resting-place —no accurate records of the slain are kept.

¶ In Germany, today, no bands play in the public parks; all savings-banks are closed; commercial banks pay or not, as the War Minister orders; all insurance-companies—both life and fire—are bankrupt; colleges are turned into hospitals—

all students are at the front; factories are closed; laboratories are but memories.
❡ All the progress of the last forty-three years lies a jumbled, tumbled mass of fears and tears in the dust and dirt of the gladiatorial arena.
All the wealth gained in that forty-three years is already lost, dissolved in a mulch of festering human flesh.

———

CALIGULA, that royal pagan pervert, was kind compared with the Kaiser.
❡ Nero, the fiddling fiend, with his carelessness in the use of fire, never burned property in all his pestilential career worth one-half that destroyed when the Kaiser's troops applied the torch to storied Louvain.
❡ What has been done before may be done again. The " Thirty Years' War " reduced Germany to cannibalism. The old and the

11

crippled were knocked on the head and eaten ❧ ❧

The nunneries were turned into communes. Nuns, widows, girls, were seized and distributed like cattle. Every soldier was ordered to take two wives, because the country must be repopulated.

Women and children toiled in the fields like beasts of burden to raise crops to feed the people.

Family-names were lost, destroyed, forgotten ❧ ❧

A new order prevailed.

To commemorate the dead was a crime ❧

———

WHY do the German people stand by the War-God?

The answer is easy. It is a matter of the hypnotic spell of patriotism and the lure of the crowd, combined with coercion ❧

We make a virtue of the thing we are compelled to do.

The marvelous recuperative power of the Teutonic people is proved by the fact that the German race was not wiped out of existence long ago, like the Incas or the Aztecs. The will to live was strong, and a new race was ours.

Are we to go back to that black night of bloody medievalism?

Surely not! Our hearts are with Germany —the Germany of invention, science, music, education, skill—but not with the War-God. The Emperor does not represent the true Germany. He symbols the lust of power, the thirst for blood.

He is a maniacal Night-Watchman—drunk on power—who thinks he owns the factory.

⁋ The crazy Kaiser will not win. The wisdom of the world backs the Allies, and Saint Helena awaits. It must be so.

Germany will not be subjugated, but she will be relieved of a succubus that has threatened her very existence.

Disarmament must come.

This awful chain of wars will make a World Federation a necessity. It need not longer be argued for. Not a sane man or woman on earth but knows World Federation and disarmament mean the safety of the race.

Canada and the United States have kept the peace for a hundred years, by " an arrangement " whereby it was provided that each government should have on the Lakes two boats each with a crew not to exceed twenty-six men.

The " arrangement " has worked.

Statesmen must be businessmen, not soldiers. Statesmen build a State—soldiers destroy it.

One army and one navy, serving as police,

14

can keep the peace. ⟪ Beyond this, " preparedness " spells hell in italics.

Let us thank William the Second for exploding for us, among other bombs, the bromidial fallacy that vast armaments insure peace.

When things get bad enough they tend to cure themselves.

The Law of Compensation is at work. At the close of this war, which famine will dictate shall be brief, there will be for sale a fine job-lot of secondhand crowns.

And the forces of industry, economy, invention, harmony, science and friendship shall rule the world.

⟪ We believe in the Germany of Beethoven, Goethe and Schiller— not in the Prussia of Nietzsche, Trietschke and Bernhardi.

Violence,

as a corrective for

commercial jealousy,

is scarcely good

economics

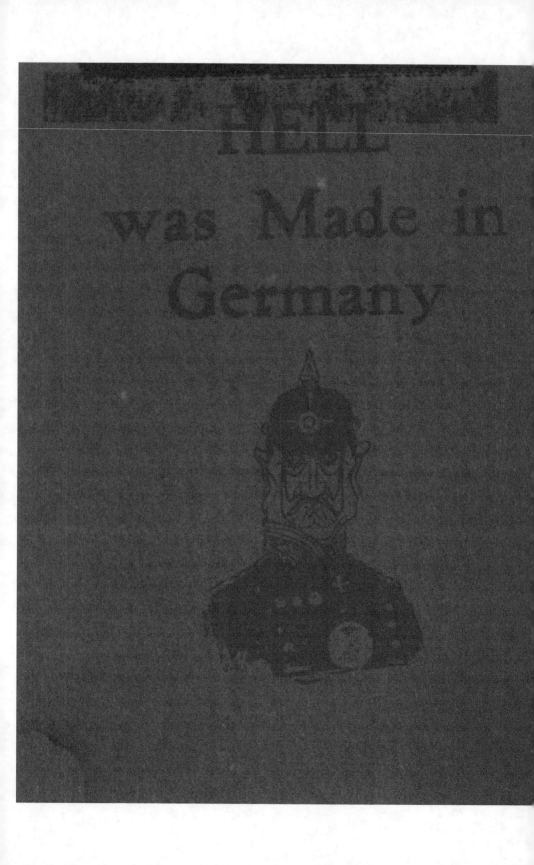